SUPERDOOM

Published by Tin House, Portland, Oregon

Distributed by W. W. Norton & Company

Library of Congress Cataloging-in-Publication Data

Names: Broder, Melissa, author.
Title: Superdoom : selected poems / Melissa Broder.
Description: Portland, Oregon : Tin House, [2021]
Identifiers: LCCN 2021001869 | ISBN 9781951142650
   (paperback) | ISBN 9781951142667 (ebook)
Subjects: LCGFT: Poetry.
Classification: LCC PS3602.R6345 S87 2021 | DDC 811/.6—dc23
LC record available at https://lccn.loc.gov/2021001869

Poems from *When You Say One Thing but Mean Your Mother*
appear with permission from Ampersand Books

Poems from *Meat Heart* and *Scarecrone* appear with permission
from Publishing Genius Press

First US Edition 2021
Printed in the USA
Interior design by Jakob Vala

www.tinhouse.com

SUPERDOOM

selected poems

MELISSA BRODER

 TIN HOUSE, Portland, Oregon

to my father

CONTENTS

from SCARECRONE

from LAST SEXT

INTRODUCTION

As of today, March 26, 2021, I no longer know how to write a poem. I have no idea how I wrote the poems in this book.

In some ways, this state of unknowing is exciting. A poetry teacher of mine once said, quoting the poet Muriel Rukeyser, "You need only be a scarecrow for poems to land on." Perhaps, then, my amnesia as to how I made these poems indicates that I've been, at times, a scarecrow: a landing place, a vessel, a channel for poems. I like that. To me, it seems preferable to be a channel than what I usually am: a self-will-er, a scrambler, a filler of holes, a looker in "glittery shitdoors" for love (as I note in the poem "Man's Search for Meaning").

To be a channel is great, actually. To be a channel is to be reminded that I do not need to struggle to fill the holes inside with anything glittery. It is to be reminded that I actually like going inside the holes. I just keep forgetting I like it in there.

As a daily reminder that I actually do like the holes, I've been reciting the Prayer of Saint Francis for sixteen years. The first line of the prayer asks that I be made a channel, so my attention is directed right away to that emptiness as something ideal.

The prayer asks for a lot of other things too: that *where there is hatred, I may bring love*; that *where there is wrong, I may bring the spirit of forgiveness*, and other challenging aspirations for a human like me. As I note in the title of my poem "The Saint Francis Prayer Is a Tall Order," the Saint

Francis Prayer really is a tall order. But I'd like to think that when it comes to the channel part, some of these poems are a reflection of my prayers. I mean, I don't want to be a spiritual materialist. But all of these poems were written between 2006 and 2016—at the height of my Saint Francis Prayer-ing. So, maybe.

I also like framing my amnesia as to the creation of these poems in terms of mystery. Mystery is an element I've always loved about poetry: the space a poem makes for the unknown. In a time where certitude is very trendy (maybe it was always trendy, but it feels especially hot now), I love that a poem can be a vessel for living in the questions themselves, a sphere of ambiguity, a celebration of negative capability, a field for beginner's mind, a braid of darkness and light, a little fortress of sacred pause.

Reader, do not doubt that you can fully experience these poems without "understanding" them intellectually or drawing any conclusions about them. I invite you to do whatever you want with them, of course. But know that I am re-experiencing them now without understanding how they happened.

And yet, it has always been my fear as an artist that one day I will just lose it. This *it*ness is hard to define, but it involves the muse, the gift, the way, the talent, the ability, the inspiration, the craft; any multitude of *it*s, really, intrinsic to creation.

Creative friends tell me this is not possible. You cannot just lose it. Sure, sometimes when you turn on the proverbial creative sink, a little rust comes out. But it's just a question of leaving the faucet on long enough to let the rust run out. Then, the pure water comes.

Still, I lack faith in the inevitability of pure water. And when I look at these poems and do not know how I wrote them, or if I would have the capacity to write a strong poem again, I feel concerned. What will disappear next?

In all fairness to the faucet, the Muses, and I guess, to myself, I haven't been actively writing poems since the last of these were written in 2016. I have since turned to the dark side, which is to say, I have been writing prose.

When I lived in New York City, I used to write my poems on the train. I am a perfectionist, hard on myself, and so I've always preferred to write my first drafts while in motion or in a place where I'm not supposed to be writing (like a funeral), rather than at an "official writing place" like a desk. This is because I need to trick the critic within me into letting a first draft just be whatever it is. If I don't encourage messiness and imperfection, there will be no first draft at all.

In the fall of 2013, I left New York and moved to Los Angeles—not for the sake of my writing, but because of my partner's health. In LA, I could no longer write poems while in transit. It's just not safe to be typing up poems while driving on the 405. Instead, I found myself dictating words into my phone using Siri and a free notes app while I drove. The geographic change, and resulting dictation, altered my writing. My line breaks disappeared. The language became more conversational. What was once poetic output became essays. The essays became a book called *So Sad Today*.

During this time, I completed the poems that appear in *Last Sext*. But after *Last Sext*, my remaining poetic energies were redirected as I dictated the first draft of my novel *The Pisces*. While *The Pisces* celebrates Sappho, and hopefully, at its best, resonates with the rhythm and music of lyric poetry, it is decidedly prose.

The writing of prose finally allowed me—in my mid-thirties—to become a full-time writer, able to support myself on writing alone. Let's be honest, poetry doesn't make it rain. And I love that these poems were absent of profit motive. Did I write them to survive? Yes. But the survival was psychological and spiritual, rather than a question of putting food on my table. I was always a poet with a day job.

When I look back over these selected poems, I see the same psychospiritual and mythopoetic themes that inspire my prose writing. We write our obsessions, and mine seem to be—in these poems and now in prose—sex, death, consumption, god, spiritual longing, earthly longing, and holes. It's nice to know that being able to eat off my creations hasn't changed my preoccupations. But, when art and commerce mix, there is inevitably another internal critical voice that joins the chorus of internal voices appraising our text. The voice says, "Can I eat off this?" In these poems, that voice was beautifully silent.

This brings me to the one element that I do remember about the creation of these poems. It isn't a process, or a craft note, but a feeling. Many nights, I wrote on the subway between 137th Street in Manhattan and Hoyt Street in Brooklyn. I remember feeling, at times, during that commute, like I was disappearing in the best of ways. On these rides, flying through the darkness of the tunnels, I would become obsessed with a piece of a particular poem I was working on: a syllabic beat, or finding the perfect word.

On the subway, I would disappear into rhythmic counting or the hunt for the word. I would forget that I was riding in a subway car. In a way, I was no longer riding in a subway car but riding in a poem. This is the best kind of vanishing. This is my favorite transcendence.

It would be my joy, reader, if you find in some of these poems a bit of transcendence for yourself. I wish for you only the very best kind of vanishing. If you need respite from the body, I hope you get it. If you need freedom from the space-time continuum, that too. I won't even mention the 24-hour news cycle.

At the very least, I hope you enjoy a few of these poems, once written by someone, who I'm told is me.

—Melissa Broder

FROM

WHEN YOU SAY ONE THING BUT MEAN YOUR MOTHER

PRAYER OF THE TEENAGE WAIFS

We want security and we want out!
The groceries have cobwebs. French toast sticks
and sickie chicken sausages turn lettuce
for breakfast. Put dinner in a locket,
then sniff to get to clavicle heaven
where Mommy gets pinched and shock treatments
are ice capades, Sweet'N Low sensations

of Fatherland. Oh Fatherland! She's been
a bad babysitter. Deliver us
from Burger King with *People* magazine.
Let the basement be our basement, the bones
and ringtones our only breath in mirrors;
let mammaries unbloom, let fumes be food
and we'll massacre into cylinders.

UNHITCHERY

Soon Ann Simons runs me backward down the street,
pee running up my leg. Soon we unsqueak

the bedsprings while your Ma lies next door, absorbed
in her Corinthians. Soon. Soon I drop out

of my own poem; the skull on the wall
reverts into an antelope, its heart

itching for the woods. Soon the incense sticks
unburn, the air conditioner returns

to Carrier's brainstorm soon. Soon the street
crosses a car, *The White Album* comes before

Rubber Soul, the L train stuffs itself
in Canarsie. Soon you get hungry

for what you never used to have. The star
of *Mamma Mia!* stops the music

and says: *When I was a child I didn't get
enough attention. Okay, I got too much*

attention. Soon the accident happens
after the news. Andy Warhol stays

dead. The mouth pours the mead. Soon the cars
are beaten by the horses rusting.

THE TALL LADY NEVER NOT DOING LAUNDRY

Always inhaling Sunlight,
Dynamo, Ultra or Bold.
Reducing fading, fighting
for the bright! Double concentration:
what could be more refreshing?

Never again press close in winter
coats to taste him of Marlboro
and Rumple Minze, breathing through his nose.

Always going vacationing
on an Arm & Hammer; the whitest
whites looking light, while advances
in science inspire undies
to live happier lives.

Never again thrown down and splayed
good on the city soccer field,
rubbing against his mushrooming.

Always hearing the humming
of the robust spinning tubs.
Non-corrosive stainless steel
is powerful, but gentle,
for an evening of tumbling.

Never again hump his hands
and clutch findings, murmuring
'no stopping' and meaning it.

Always sudsing in hot water
with double stain-lifter, folding
sheets and hanging jeans. Cotton
won't shrink from the quickening friction.
Fluff it, pat it, crease and repeat.

YOUR MOTHER IS DYING AND I WANT DETAILS

Now she's getting closer.
When you call, I salivate

for updates, last regrets,
the stench, a cellular

twinkling: not enough
battery power left

to run radio, spiders
of unbeing, as if

through some aperture
you will catapult me

underneath her skin
to walk the girders

of her skeleton
and I'll be the next

to know what.

UNDER THE DM TONIGHT

The other side of good health
is gravy, I'm certain,
as Mom slips me the rectal

and sips of Robitussin
cherry suspension,
already surfing the wake

of a *Price is Right-*
Lite-Brite-Sudafed
jag. It's the end

of the old I AM,
a brand new –ism. Pray
it doesn't fade in minutes.

There are many medicines
for the taking
but just a few will take.

Grown-ups all get head transplants;
only pity ice creams
for me and my starlike ache.

TRADITION

When we get hitched there will be no cake feed,

no first dance to *Feeling I'm Falling*,
no bandmaster announcing our entrance

as Mr. and Mrs. X. *The thing
about tradition*, said a very married friend,
you only get one chance to do it big.

When we divorce we will be a part
of an American tradition,
a grand incision. How will it feel
to live in the percentages? Don't be afraid

of blue days, ghostly fridges. Pain is
the touchstone of progress, and this tradition
we can really sink our teeth in, do it twice
or three times even, maybe with each other

like Taylor and Burton. On the good years
we'll invite our lawyers over for Scrabble
and Kung Pao chicken. On the off years we'll
call each other to check in. *How is*

the loneliness? I watch Letterman.
I miss your glasses. I miss kissing
off all of your lipstick. We'll compare

dates and complain about therapists.
She called me manic. So many Republicans.

I miss your applesauce. I miss your night sweats.

WHO LOVES YA?

When the three poet ancestors, each named
Ann, fold me into their Bloomsbury Group
at a rooftop pool party, there's not
enough oxygen. They talk old guard—
jazz, ashtray, verb, Paris—and warn
against falling into fashion.

What if I don't take snifters? I ask.
Nowadays, Diet Coke's ok, says Ann.
I didn't try sweet vermouth, I say.
It's never too late in the day, says Ann.
Take a break from your scares, says Ann.
Or have them anthologized, says Ann.

The Anns' daughters emerge from behind
a plate of poached pears to tell me I'm blessed.
The Anns aren't jealous of my youth.
Look, they say, *none of them wear bathing suits.*
I think they must like me for my womb,
how it's pruned like theirs. But the Anns know

my first baby before I do.
Expensive and confusing, says Ann.
Symbiotic and fattening, says Ann.
It'll be no Ars Poetica, says Ann.

KING JAMES APPROXIMATELY

Lately I'm practicing practicing god's will,
not my own, like the lusty astronaut

who drove a two-pound hammer drill from Houston
to Orlando, wearing a diaper

so she wouldn't have to pull over
before kidnapping her lover's wife.

I didn't think I'd live long enough
to see me still being me, but Saturn

returns with a teenage trick: steal packages
of fake meat from the deli counter and count

the slices aloud; then eliminate them
out the window of a speeding car, each piece

a gamey hood ornament: bologna
Jetta, ham Corolla, smoked turkey taxi.

How should I know god's will? I'm making choices
on crumpled pieces of fake meat tossed in the air.

In the old days, I knew it on my father's face
when he saw the bologna car, turned to me and stared.

FROM
MEAT
HEART

MEAT HEART

Listen wormhead
There is no celery emergency
No rutabaga for alarm
No evil peach in your vein of air
Or pomegranate on high alert
Though kiwi seeds may streak the soil
And tubers crop up bruised
And cornhusk filaments
Still jacket tongues
There is only Slim Jim love
And taco glow
And all-night burger magic

BONES

I held a nightlight
to my bones.

Run run said the moon
or build yourself
a rowboat with a roof.

I am like a sailor
who is terrified of fish

if I see a skeleton
I might begin

to vomit up
the mystery
and then what?

I am nothing
like a sailor.

CHAMPIONSHIP

God keeps unfurling me
with god's gigantic helium.
There are scratchmarks all over
my life.   That's from my mitts.
Other human,   this unfurliness
is far too spacious.   Would you
lend me some muscle?   Let's
write a sermon on control. Let's
write a love song for heavyweights
and by heavyweights
I mean everyone.

PENNSYLVANIA PRAYER

Bless me I was once myself and couldn't read
a thermostat. My mother's breasts were long

inside her bathrobe. (Sometimes we were Polish.)
I believe god knows these things about me

so I needn't say them with heart. I'm afraid
to say anything with heart. One summer

there came an ice storm and a skinny lady
flew inside my ear. She forced me to eat

grapes, only grapes, until I wasn't
myself anymore. Wine made me feel myself.

Wine made me somebody else. God knows
there is more to this story. My heart fell out.

SUPPER

Boy comes to me at a church potluck
perfumed with frankincense and lasagna.

He believes I am a gentle bird girl
in my tulip sweater and raincoat.

I am not so gentle, but I act as if
and what I act as if I might become.

He says *Let's be still and know refreshments.*
Tater tot casserole is wholesome fare.
Let's get soft, let's get really, really soft.

I do not say *I am frightened of growing plump*;
something about the eye of a needle
and sidling right up close to godliness.

Instead I dig in,
stuff myself on homemade rolls,
chicken pie and cream chipped beef with noodles.

I eat until my bird bones evanesce.
I eat until I bust from my garments.

I become the burping circus lady
with meaty ham hocks and a sow's neck.

Boy says *Let's get soft, even softer.*
We vibrate at the frequency of angel cake.

Our throats fill with ice cream glossolalia.
The eye of the needle grows wider.
There is room at the organ bench.

I play.

SUPERDOOM

There are 200 flavors of panic,
the worst is seeing with no eyes.
Cowboys call it riding your feelings.
I call it SUPERDOOM.
On April 5th I was 98% alive.
I saw my blood sugar at the mall
and spilled into a hall of numb light.
The earth kept coming and coming.
Every human was a baby
puncturing my vehicle.
I tried to stuff a TV
in the hole where prayer grows.
A salesman prescribed zen.
I said *How long have you been alive?*
He said *Six minutes.*

BINGE EATING IN 2067

Wild Man is just like me
starved into fractions.

We all are, the whole colony
raised on motherboards

sugar cane screenshots
pixelated onions.

But I have a jaw that seeks chunks
and he has the heart of a fat man.

In his cave we drink vapor ale
snarf dust fowl, sediment meats.

Nothing is enough
he chains me to the rocks

then slaps my growling stomach
until I spew static

making space for ash fish
and elemental octopi.

I find a thighbone in the stone
and think of friends gone missing.

I hear my human heart beat.
I wonder why he has utensils.

When he cooks a real live cassoulet
flesh and fat, no hoax,

I turn my face from the bowl
and put my fingers in his mouth.

AHOY!

By the gates of the walled lung
we stand circled in the dark.

We've come through his throat
by ship.

I say *What if he hiccups?*

I am channeling my grandmom's fears
of common colds and foreign air.
The women judge me silly.

They say *Unsisterly!*
Your angst is old, so old.

To prove myself fierce
I run down the danger corridor
of his guts to his intestines.

There are cabbages and acid.
There are meat screams
and a fancy market.

I am relieved to discover
my favorite gourmet yogurt
with full nutrition labeling.

Indulging in a blueberry variety
on the banks of his duodenum
I watch the villi sway.

It's a scene nearing Monet's *La Rivière*
but I am not a visual person.

My mind is full of letters.

I say *Help me be a sister.*
I mean to say *Don't make me die alone.*

Back at the lung
roommates have been chosen.

MIKVEH

Monthly I must snort the universe

    or seduce a hummingbird

betrothed to a ladybird

acclaimed for her art

    a sculptor with clay on her pants

(ugly pants)

don't you understand

    I will not go to god

for milk again.

    Wreck your nest

turn red

make me goddamn seafood soup, bird

    cook intimately with clams

on counter and blood on wall

    spoon me up

that ocean broth

I must be rid of this medusa feeling

    or else

feel my forehead

say *not so scarlet*

    not so evil

and flannel nightclothes

will grow backwards

    over my arms

an arm-based piety.

DE FOREST STATION

She was built with forest brain
so she would learn to say
I know nothing about forests.

It is the geniusest thing
a treehead girl can say
this I know nothing.

She tried to be a DDTberry.
She tried killsyrups.

She did not think another
treehead girl would ever come
but here they are
with matching forests.

Now there are two.
A map might be made.

Come canopy you
DDTberry killsyrup treeheads.
Let's action the kind word
tongue to tree.

Let us fertilize
root and branch.
Let us make map us
and learn to say *help me.*

Help me help me help me
until we go fallow
clean to our unearthliness.

Let us say *help me*
until the cackle crows are stilled.

Help me help me help me.
help me help me help me.

It is the heroist thing
a treehead girl can say.

WATERFALL

The most romantic thing a human being can say
to another human being is *Let me help you vomit.*
No human being has ever said this to me
and I keep going to god too clean as though god
is frightened of muddy feet. If I am missing
a hairpin I don't go at all. Please describe
your vomiting; it is like a psalm to me
a place where wilderness might be new.
Other people's dirt makes a lovely frock.
Grant I be forgiven in the gush.

MEGACHURCH

The holy men want me
Swooning drunk
They say *If you feel like nonsense*
Get nonsenser
If you feel bananas
Make a sundae already

Oh I do
I want holiness to meet me halfway
Meet me easy
Like a tugboat on glitter water
Hotel music
Ultragloss

So easy to fall in the water
How easy these holy men come on
Bodies of soap
With pinwheel erections
They eat hamburgers effortlessly
Only some have hips

It is movie night
In their church in America
A crucifixion movie
No a movie about love
They offer me megaCokes
With rum

Rum will make the movie
More romantic
I cannot say
I am undrunk
How I got to be undrunk
Not here

Boredom is going to get crucified here
The whole church is beeping
Glitter water
Glitter rum
Even my nail polish
Beeping.

STEAK NIGHT

In husbandland I am made
of hamburger, eggs and potatoes

a food brew really
scraps spackled.

A kitchen swells around
full of cakes and clocks

and babydolls not like ham.
A hash has happened

the husband is absent
my marriage dress hangs

by the stove.
I put me in my mouth

to taste patty melts
stripey fats and underblood

juicy dregs for geraniums.
I could let drops

and grow victory gardens.
Might I cleave a piece to suck?

O the eggs are growing old
or else they're growing lungs.

RAISE YOUR HAND IF YOU'RE SURE

I want to be a child of happy illusion
not sad illusion or truth. All the vehicles
I've used to make the road stop rippling
stopped working. I bought a blue bicycle
with a shovel on back. Nothing stayed buried.
I'm told to sit and watch the road until
a light shines on my condition. That asylum
seems so broken I can't find the sitting.
I don't feel like a tree in the rain.
I feel like an old groccry trading
in fear. I want medicine quick,
the unity that so terrifies me
to begin a strong new cycle
and everybody scared
of feeling can
come spin.

GOOD HOUSEKEEPING

Red was coming through the walls.
Red dribbled on the carpet.
The damask used to be black.
I asked Kate if she'd gotten
her menses on the carpet.
She was sick of my attitude.
Her friend Audre would come over
to tell me I was awful.
They'd revoke my Sappho card.
Save it, sister, save it
for Susan B. Anthony.
She'll be the judge of menses.
She'll be the judge of carpets.

Served me right about the house.
It was done in mother's style.
Now it was a Jell-O mold
cherry with floating fruit.
I couldn't make anything float.
I couldn't make anything boil.
I'd been seeing boys on the sly
but only to test them with forks,
never to coagulate.
Was it all my undoing?
How awful I thought I was.
It dribbled on the carpet,
it was coming through the walls.

LACK

I found the Summer of Love in a trash can at Hardee's &
    I ate it.
I found it snaked under a gluten-sensitive thickburger,

a big hot ham 'n cheese & a side salad. You want
    revolution?
That's another trip. I only know what it feels like to eat

the Summer of Love & what it feels like for this body, a
    body
lashed by machines. I have two desk machines, a lap
    machine

& a talk machine. I have a hair machine & a sex machine.
I have a machine for acting as if, a machine for duck & run

& a machine to knock your socks off. I have always
    cherished
my machines & I have always cherished not thinking

about anybody other than my body, but ever since I ate
the Summer of Love I have not stopped dreaming of babies.

WHEN ENVY WENT TO DIE

I could not believe what a cinnamon feeling
this starlet gave me.   I was not dwarveg
                    nor rendered mammoth.
I felt like a whole dot   a good dot.

It was as if somebody twirled heather ribbon
over my frontal lobe.
                    Now I could just sit back
and eat corned beef   for the rest of my life.
                    Her beauty was a spoon in space.
                                Feed me, I said.

I kept waiting for a monkey inside my brain
to bring me down
                    but this was not amphetamine
                    and no shadow thoughts befell me.

I mean it when I say love entered
                                through my eyes
Lift mine eyes   & keep lifting mine eyes.

She was thc wild opus of a starlet machinist.
                    I am proud of our being.
Sometimes it goes light inside late.   I say
congratulations!

DRIVE-IN

We've all been miscast   do you know
who put us in this crazy film?

Until the end, we say.   *I thought it
        such an awful script until the end.*

            We could forget we were born
but our mothers are streaked
                            into our hearts.

            It's like some other mother
tossed our magic glasses to the dahlias.

Let's show up for this thing   anyhow
in color.

            Blessed is the celluloid species
                and blessed is the popcorn.

HYDROPONICS

He said *drop your notebook
the temple is everywhere.*

He said a magic mushroom
would eliminate tennis nose
and lend feather atmosphere.

We dropped the drop.
Chimney memory
oceaned away.

I felt like a holiday pumpkin.
We were very sweater
holding thicket vigil
until plants curled.

In a different version
we remained in the rift
between breath and vision
and we're still under that flap.

In this version we exited
to confront a restaurant.
I got touchy
about ranch dressing.

He knew how to take a staircase
from stem to lesson.

I made it about object itself:
stem and mushroom.

I couldn't stop
collecting spores.

I was shoehorning
stamens into a container
trying to architect
the whole diorama.

My arms were like cupboards.
I wouldn't let go of the pipe.

He pointed to the staircase
and I said *ethanol*.

I put him in a locker
and entered the grain range.

It was cannibal tundra.
I was conductor.

My eye was a centimeter
but I never drank
a pink girl drink.

BYE

When I die I regret the dieting
and literary theory. I am just
oh my god one raspberry left. Strange
how we had different experiences.
I would love to have handed you toilet paper
under a stall door. I was thinking with my head
and forgot about my hands. I also regret
the obsessing over ragged seams.
Funny thing is: sometimes the obsessing
called attention to itself doing it
while it did it. I guess we could have gone
naked. Do you know the story of Helen?

TODAY I WILL BE A BENEVOLENT NARRATOR

My little paper people
I am going to love you

Though I do not yet love myself
I ask god for help

I say god, you old stuffed potato
These characters need a yellow kitchen

These characters need a hot dinner
Help me help them

Pull my strings
And I'll even join them at the table

Maybe you will join us too?
Someone else

Can pull your strings
You are tired

You must be so tired
Let's be happy peasants together.

H1N1

Back from the flu today
so in love with power.

I wore a paper nightie
over crinoline slippers

ghost nuns soaped my surfaces
and grunted

we wish you could see
how not awful you are

dear sisters devoted only
to helping me vomit

prayer candles
on an avalanche level

I forgot my dialect
of defects entirely

a furry creature
carcassed at the altar

I felt so righteous
I humped a humidifier

climaxed on the linens
dropped dead in tongues

a guilty future chimed
but my tea read *stay*

be not a saint
be queasy

confessing nothing
to a slice of honeyed toast

I was so touched
what I heard myself say.

MR. BUBBLE

I controlled my words, my deeds and nothing more.
God wanted no revenge on my body.

I was afraid to do good will for my body
or I might vanish. I was a child and you were too.

Let us bathe each other and exact revenge.
Everybody needs a lot of fathers.

When I am father I will sew us curtains
made of other men's voices, first a patch then a moan.

Sometimes the curtains will come between us.
Mostly they will be around us.

When you are father you will build me a hardhat
with a light in it. I will not be afraid of light.

I will feel my muscles under me
like good pavement. Beauty won't kill me in the street.

Then will come a silence over every house
and every town, a year of it but up.

In the air among the insects, our first bodies
and everything we don't know about physics.

FAUNA

They called it a meat prayer
blood bubbles to heaven.
We would roast Mr. White
with cherries on a spit
by the ocean.

They promised me
pina colada.

They promised the meal
would suffocate
all memory
until I screamed
dear rabbit god!

But I remember everything
the evening's fabric
lacking candles
no sense of orchid

how I said
I would rather dream
of Jerusalem
than go
to Jerusalem
over his gumbo ribs.
Oh drumless air!
Oh garbage food!

No more feathers
than boiler chicken
no more ascension
than sweetbreads.

I split his lip for figs
and lit a limb
but I am still
carrying my head.

FROM

SCARECRONE

ASTRAL LOCKET

She went into the silent room
and in the silent room there had never been a word
only the breath before the word

and she was deep within herself
her own breathing and the breathing of the world
the Earth swelling and pumping

thick blank in all canals
elevating her entire body
then vanishing her completely

and it felt good to be bodiless
in this pre-word vanishing

then she was offered up the men
one for each of the rest of her days
with their middle fingers and axes
hymnbones and ligaments

the men who meant an end to vanishing

for in the silent room
one must return all gifts
to make room for other gifts

a light for blood exchange

the chance to float in different ways
than the silence already floated her
which was already
so good

WHEN I HEAR THE WORD *SERENITY* I THINK *DOPED*

I am told to sit and wait for it
in the liturgy of moths
like there is even a choice
like if I called it would eclipse
my sad sack of dark words
no it would not
no it would not
every time I called it came
but not like a thunderhead
not the lasers I expected
always peoplewords
or some piece of person ripped sideways
sideways spirit
below as above
and no one is watching
but please believe it cares
I must believe it cares and cares
as hurt dots the sod
let my tongue unravel
to lick a milky cord
even as I waste my minutes
let me cream the cord
right to my heart
with syllable and spit
though it will never be what I want

and I am going to have to resemble me
as I came into this desert
broken up
and full of bones
like the universe is too big
to be seen all at once
like the whale was already written
like ok there is a light
but I cannot feel the nod
I will not get to feel the nod
and if I feel the nod
it isn't it

THE GREAT

This is a conversation
I am conversing with The Great
Though I know no perfect talk exists
And if it does I will never talk perfect
I talk with snow in my mouth
I talk with snakes in my mouth
There are many greater mouths than mine
Can we still be friends?
Volition me to The Great!
I seek in garbage doors
This strange seeking is not without reason
For The Great has made a million dark and slimy charms
My palms are full of slimy cargo
I am carving my way to The Great
I am carving through my slimy body
When it breaks The Great floods in

HOW TO GIVE HEAD TO A SICK PERSON

I am going to grow you from a bean
and anything that I grow shall be mine
I will suck you from a bean
and I will suck you into a horn
and I will spell out i a m h e a l i n g y o u
I will do it with my tongue
this is not all I will do
but it is the last of my words
there have been so many words
falling over us like paper cutouts
there has been great disappointment
but here we are now
my elbows jut like strong wings
I am a very strong girl
look at what a woman you have
I am the priestess of resurrection
though I cannot make your body strong
I will make your heart loud
your heart is already so brave
you have given me so much power
you are my mother and my father
I am your dog and your daughter
look at how we are still alive
the clock is dead under the floor
and you go in the dark cavern of my mouth

and you go in the dark recesses of my mind
and you go and you go and you go and you go
and you go and you go and you go and you go

SATISFY THE DESOLATE

I call it sex
because I don't know
how else to say *terrified of dying*.
Silence ruins
everything. It says:
you will not get your wings this way
not the wings you want
and you want
more than anybody.
I have wanted
many unfair things.
What is most unfair
is that the Earth is still okay
with me being here
I think, and even
encourages it.
Hello ocean
you have asked me
not to die, but I swim
in neon pools
that are happy
to kill me.

LIGHT CONTROL

I have never been inside myself
Another place wants me dead
It is built in a ring around my core
Like asking a donut how to live
It can only cry and be eaten
Don't you see
Angels have tried to help me
And I smiled for them
Feeling genuinely good and kind
Then after a while I got tired
Of being on good behavior
They never asked for perfection
But I felt I needed to perform
And the smile stayed no matter what I did
Even when dying improperly
I left everyone I knew in the other room
But I picked them back up again
Teach me to die teach me to die
I want to create a beautiful dying
The end will need to be dark and soft
Like walking home to your real mother

HI HUMANITY

I was
scared
my soul
would
never
call and
now it is
calling
and I
am like
shhhh

POWER NOTHING

When I say I am a fierce woman I mean I am a gentle woman.

When I say I am a gentle woman I mean leave me alone.

When I say leave me alone I mean I don't know what to do.

When I say I don't know what to do I mean HELP.

When I say HELP I mean I believe in something bigger.

When I say I believe in something bigger I mean because I
   want to.

When I say because I want to I mean because I need to.

When I say because I need to I mean to live.

MUD RUSH

I have new commandments to help me love the wilderness
First commandment: never leave the wilderness
Make a fire or beget an image

I beget the fallen angel Azazel
We are kissing in a ditch
He cries for banging up his mother's heart

Every woman is the same woman
Azazel's mother is his wife
Who am I?

I can make tattoos out of berry juice and sticks
I tattoo crosses on Azazel's fingers
I make them so they look like anchors

Azazel sinks his anchor fingers in
I turn sapphire blue
His hands will not stay hooked

I stuff my holes with sticks
Then I burn down the wilderness
I burn mosquitos and flies

I burn wolfshit and trees
Azazel begins to choke in firelight
In this way he rises

DIRT NAP

Azazel's dead body rose
because Azazel was never
alive. I am alive
and this is also about me.
Highly sensitive persons
are angels. Let's give a shoutout
to softness. Humans please touch me
until I grow an adapter.
Fetch my dopamine blanket
the moon is in Aries
is in crisis. Azazel rose.
Azazel was colored bright orange.
The nozzle they twist on your lips
when you die makes your spirit
arcade off its hinges.
The body turns colors
that a spirit underneath
your spirit always wanted
to be. Azazel was
cantaloupe. Azazel was
tangerine. Break my spirit
I say break it now on a grave
or over the edge of
a casket. You will see it
was only a blemish.

THE NATURE OF OUR CONCERNS

This is a fire, a fire of learning
to die. Fuel the fire with no objects
specific to one generation
just a pyre of sitting
in the collected whispers
of all who have lived. Allow them
to frighten you with their having passed
and still keep sitting. Don't reach
for any clothes or tattoos,
you are always naked anyway
and yes you do
have angel wings
that grow heavy with love
sometimes. Love is all the time
if you are quiet. How much
are you quiet?

LIVING DOWNERS

Please don't call me out
I am getting worse
quiet fucks me good
but I can't hear
I make fake people in my serrated brain
and eat them with my one free mouth
their bones are tar
to fill me with no needle
the Buddha shakes his head
I hand him my holes
he drapes them over his shoulders
sits on the sky
the dust and sunlight
the pine trees and the fucking moon
if he can be still then good
if he can awaken then good
I am already growing more holes
and will not do the wait
in the temple of my jaw
I do not claim to be right
I am a lone wolf
I am a lonely wolf
I make people up
and I eat them

SHINY EYES

The difference between love and _____ is makebelieve.

Reality has meat but I don't care.

I sit with illusion for six days.

On the seventh day god calls me lost from within.

The god of love is maybe over me.

I hear the sky shut.

The god of love never gets over anyone.

I am the god of love.

You have to keep falling out.

I am so full of eyes I am going blind.

In the dark the god of love can find me.

Does it have to be silent?

I am going to go alltheway dark.

I think I am still holding on.

Even dead I am still here.

Even dead the light.

THE SAINT FRANCIS PRAYER IS A TALL ORDER

Mostly it's hard to believe
what matters is in your heart.
I'll remember for an hour.
I'd like to tell god what god's will is.
I'd like for god to make god's tongue
really fast and gentle on my—
sorry if this isn't scripture.
I tried / I'm tired
and I ate up all the begats.
To be a saint is to be courageous
about the pursuit of what?
I have a pretty mouth.
Meet me at the black clock.

JUDGMENT

When the preacher comes to town I try to hump the preacher
I try to hump angels
I cannot untouch sublime beings

My guardian angels are mine and all for me
When they leak they leak me
Still there are cracks between us
And you have to fill up cracks with candy

If I am not allowed candy I use my body
If I am not allowed my body I use the internet
Television is going to deliver me from the internet
The angels pray over my screens

My angels are probably lonely
Also disillusioned with me
I have always felt the presence of a disappointed being

The preacher says I am not dead
I am definitely dying
I am already digging out of my coffin

I dress in cicada skins
I go bright blonde
Above me is the blonde angel Raphael
And I try to make the blonde angel french me

The blonde angel has a thick tongue
He wants to talk about healing
The violence no one has done to me

Every violence I have done to me
When I leak I leak me
What was so hell that I violenced me
That I knifed the wounds into my wings

There were always beautiful horses
There were cracks in all the horses
When I stuffed their mouths with candy
They turned to rotten

I made candy luncheons in the pasture
It tasted very desire
I poured cherry soda into all my cracks

Tell the angels to give me sugar
If they do not want to hump me
A supreme being should heal me
But only for forever

DONUT

Thirsty for milk and humping
god's knee till god feels like a doll
passed from suffering person
to suffering person.
I have never loved in a way
that wasn't gorged or object-y
but I'm getting better
at praying for all humankind
in the dawn before I eat
the sun. No god wants to be
an old man with balls down
to his knees and I don't either
I don't think. I waver because
you shouldn't just fill one space
with the unclarity of another.

PROPER DISPOSAL OF HOLY WATER

When I purge the abscess of a girlhood
I am heavier a female.
Thick lips belch the zeros
of my previous condition.
The headmistress of space and time
lavishes gravity like a bear.
You can be blessed at every altar
and a grunt in waking life
but I am one woman now
from scalp to toenails
teeth to pussy.
This new opacity makes the misplaced years
my entire education seem an imp
a hollow tool
really gone.
On to piss the fountains
bust through my smocks
in gleeful fat and torpor.
The harp of the flesh is no illusion
or phenomenon reserved for babies.
Rain in every hole
butter on each finger
in every breast a spit of felines
once you stop the search.
Don't go

to the swamps for medicine
or to the streams with eyes on elixir
but into the balm of your own robe.
After the family hatchet
the black air of schoolmates
who said serenity in withered books
miles of that river drain.

EXACT COMPOSITION IS A SECRET

Invent a fantasy to save me
and project it on another body.

I don't think I am worthy of rescue.

Humble me down so low
that this small bread
feels like an orgasm.

That is how we enjoy the world.

I see lovers
and they are not real.
I mean they are real
but my eyes are not.

Once upon a time the world rose
to meet my plasticine eyes.

The oceans flooded
and carried me away
and I said *thank you lord*
for making this possible.

Then I washed up on the shore
and had to start walking
through an island jungle again:
barefoot, pale and salty.

I cried
but not because I was lost.

I cried
because my body
was not waterlogged enough
to fall right off the bone.

A PREOCCUPATION MAY BE SHARED

I saw time fold into a carful of women and they dropped
    their
lips like husks.

I'm afraid of turning purple.

I don't want to hear any alarms under my hair.

O sanctus sanctus sanctus varicosis-minimus lolitas roseus
coralus salmonus tightest pinkest ingenue ingenue ingenue.

PINK – 1. Pale red. 2. The highest degree. 3. Prime. 4. To
    prune or
trim. 5. Beefcheeks' maiden voyage.

There is no need to be pink when another woman is
    already pink.

Jealous women jealous me into being jealouser.

If I soften I get to meet Joan of Arc.

We snow into an ashtray till she asks whose ashtray is this?

You must learn to love all the women.

I am proud of my me in Joan's hair tonight.

I am proud of my no-game.

The universe hums a dirge to clocks but so what?

Well ok I care.

I will maybe stop being of service to illusion.

I am interested in the ways that numbers fail.

Heaves of mourners form villages around the dead numerals.

At the funeral I finally find my eyes.

The game of my small coal needs drops down.

I am defrocked by prayer emergency.

The nudity is a wholesome pyre.

INFLATE THE SLIDE

Trade a man
who loves you
for language
I am addicted
to my thoughts
when our world
blows up
there is a pink bed
and two girls
sitting crosslegged
in pink smoke
meditating
on my dick
they feed him
strawberry yogurt
he gives them
chimeras

FOR THE REAL WORLD

I am waiting for somebody imaginary
to come back to me.

A woman
with supper breasts
depresses.

A man
who keeps shaving
burns me
out.

My imaginary person
never cooks an egg
but everyone else
does.

Everybody cooks an egg
even if they
don't.

I want to love in a place
that is contingent
on nothing.

I want to forge a union of nothing.

People don't want
to become
imaginary.

People are planning
trips to real places
and it's awful.

CONSECRATION

Yes I put myself here
I was having a terror time
I made a muscle
out of every trashy wing
and crawled to you
and your soft dick is shit to me
holy shit
in this way
I am sucking on your shit
I am trying to help your softshitdick
reach a miracle dimension
and I don't blame you
for being unwilling
to comply with my dream
the world is real
you are there
you like living
in the end
I don't want to make the grass
I don't want to go under it
zen is not for me
you are not for me
I hear dogs inside of me
some are good and some are wrong
I keep feeding the wrong dogs

VISIBLE WORLD

I bang
my forehead
on a thing
then go oops
the sky
it looks like
sheet rock
or a joke
it is
the sky
I am
waiting
on a stroke
maybe
chandeliers
up there
magick
is for people
who do not
believe
it all
is already
here
when
they build

a lab
that burps
goodwill
I will
worship
science

PENELOPE AND ODYSSEUS

Penelope is waiting and she is wet.
What else do we know about Penelope?
Is she braising a lamb shank to lure Odysseus?
O yeah, a lamb shank, it makes Odysseus wet.
His stomach grows heavy but he still can make rain.
He rains down on Penelope and dissolves her.
Odysseus and Penelope dissolve together.
Their stomachs are very heavy but they fly.
They fly around the whole world over every ocean.
When they fly over the deserts Odysseus laughs.
He feels he is the wettest juiciest lamb shank.
He believes he will never be dry again.
Odysseus will have to make rain again.
Odysseus will have to make rain again and again.
Odysseus's face becomes a black desert.
He asks Penelope to leave the sky.

ASK TO BE RESEATED

Dirt coat blankets the universe
and I pillow asteroid
with pervasive sense
an explosion is missing
rejection-sensitivity
soothed by palm trees
Pantheism
nice trip to CVS
vanity reasserts itself
when pain subsides
I could build a theater
around your head
perform the violence island
I was never taught to latch
I was born
latching

HAUL

Hello porn video.
Hello scarecrone
on the train.
You know we got old.
The young are devils
in our dream.
They are made of rotten sugar.
We are holding onto one car
and the car is named *tight*
like a baby. Call me
tight like a baby.
Clarity is a wart.
You see the warts
on my face? Eat them
retrospectively. Save me
scarecrone. The condition
of my face. I ate
the world and I ate
the world. It tasted
like a bandage.

VENTRILOQUISM

The gap between motherhood
and no motherhood
is grip. I wield my eggs
against women who have
dried up. Mine will dry
on a river rock, punish
my future body
for taking the river
for granted. Hold my
palms up to the Goddess
and say *Tell me what to do.*
If the Goddess wants me
knocked up I'll be a fish. If
she wants me in the river
I'll be wetter. She calls me
daughter. A man becomes
an infant in my lap.

DON'T MAKE ME GROW

A mustardseed of okayness. We're here
to know our own goodness. I have barely
cried at all. I spent so much time away
from me that when I finally feel me
I might kill me. I guess you sit
with you and see you do not kill you.
Then you live. No nothing
will give me that okayness.
I want bodies packed
around my body. A layer
is missing. The air is so
dangerous. Blink twice
you're off the path.

THE GOOD PANIC

Vortexes are pouring out
of my stomach into
my throat because: unknown.
*Don't worry, under the dying
is sadness*, says love. No
that is me talking. *Sometimes
you just get sick, even
in the mind, and there is nothing
you can do.* That is love
talking. Love, relieve me
of my fear of fear and of
my fear of everything. Do it
on your time as I know
you will. May I find you
on the internet in words
from a stranger. This is how
you work like a lattice, not
from the top down. Lay me up
so I may know my power-
lessness and therein find
my iron. Needles in my hands,
needles in my feet. Little body
pitched into the pines of having
ever been born. Big body
smeared around little body

and full of stars and horses
and fingers of everyone
who has ever touched me.
Love, you keep touching me.
Hallways of my brain filled
with wormtracks like a condom
over the light. Shitbags
in the trees. Water water
now love water water.
My mouth is wide.

MYTHIC

The universe is vacant
because I am
here.

I brought my holes and all the men
flew up inside.

What got left behind are women
who will save me.

want to lick a cosmic titty
because god built me
with these holes

so I am coming for you god

if you are the mad cow
then I am your wayward calf

if you are the mother
I say MORE LOVE NOW

and if you are the father
then bounce me on your knee
till I feel it in my holes
because that is where
I need to
feel it.

VARIETIES OF RELIGIOUS EXPERIENCE

I don't know. Humans
are always waiting for
something to stuff our
holes. Even when I have
a man in my holes I
am leaking and begging
for other. Moonlight
mushrooms. Once upon
a time I ate them and
saw the way I looked
as a baby. Light bulbs
had blue veins inside
that is how alive
everything was.
Still I wanted a man
to give me my name.
God was showing me
the code through a prism.
I fractured the glass
on purpose because
I did not want to know.

TRANSCENDENTAL CRITIQUE

As always there is schism
between skeleton
and never asking for a skeleton
tearing around the kitchen.
You enter with biscuits
and each contains a gemstone
that tastes like its color:
ruby is cherry,
pink tourmaline pussy.
The word for wish is want.
Knowledge gets us what?
Not enough biscuits.
Sick dogs sniff each other out.
I build an oven over your mouth
and set the door on fire.
Grunts are still possible.
Let's corpse.

BROTHER

How is your crown supposed to fall off
when you look like Jesus
I am superficial because it feels religious
let's light a candle for you not wanting me back
we could be dirty juice and bent crucifix
suspend the alphabet now
o sanctus sanctus sanctus puer
mea illusio mea est mea omnia
can you believe in guides your eyes can't see
can you believe I still want you
I cannot believe you would choose loneliness
loneliness is how little you want me
I know little of Christianity
so I love it
take me behind your mouth
that I might forsake it
pillar of salt
pillar of salt

LAST SKIN

I am in the hotel of bodies
temporarily. Love is
millions of needles but really
none. Dark crow, cackle cackle,
the pyramids already fell.
Leave my eye and join the light.
Don't you know I craned my neck
for saints outside. Don't you know
I felt like crying. There were bats
in my ribcage and I didn't even know.
Behind them my soul was snowing.

SKY MALL

There once was a sky full of boys.
Gravity is a vile invention
when time owns the ground.
Every field is raked with clocks.
Turnips wave a white flag.
Potatoes are bombs.
I explode them in my mirror
to fly the glass.
I fly to the leopard coast.
The scarecrone is old and dull.
Dig, she says.

SKY KIDS

You didn't know
I was unreal

I am the worst
body

nobody ever
taught me dopamine

I want to drink
your star jelly

HOPE THIS HELPS

We need a loving grownup to give us advice
and that loving grownup is the universe.
Who wants to go to the universe for help?
You can't touch the universe
or kiss its mouth
or stick your fingers in its mouth
though sometimes the universe works
horizontally through people
and I like that.
A human channeled the universe
when he said I was milk.
The human said I was born milk
but then grownups poured in lemon juice
which makes sense
because I've always felt like rotten cottage cheese
and I've been running around the planet
like I don't want to be this
when in fact I am milk
and was always milk
and will always be milk.
I don't think this is a story blaming grownups
for the ways we are ruined.
I think this is a story about knowing
what we are up against
mostly ourselves

and what our essential consistency is
which in my case is milk
and in your case is milk
you are milk you are
milk you are
so milk.

THOUSANDS

He is told to send a lock of hair
but instead sends a dossier
of charts. There are bullets,
vectors, single choice answers.
No questions. On every page
appears a yellowish husband.
The husband is a sick man.
I want the diagram-sender
sicker. I want every man
fainting in a reservoir
of contaminated water.
I have black chrysanthemums
in each hole and a loamy smell.
My climax shakes the basin.
I hold out one hand for every man
but I'm looking at my snake.

FROM A PLACE OF _____?

I opened my eyes on day 0
and said to the universe SHAKE ME
and the universe complied
which felt too real
so I built another universe
within the universe
and crawled inside

and I keep thinking
my little universe
is the only universe
but then I think no
this is not the universe at all
it is destruction

when in truth
everything is the universe
my little universe
and the big universe

and when I ask the big universe
what it wants from me
it says so easily
become a channel

but mostly I think
the universe just wants me here
so I am here
in a pain
of my making

I GIVE A CONVINCING SERMON

I give a convincing sermon. I say *The body*

is a coat. It is a very dark and heavy coat

but worthless. Mother Mary nods from the pews.

If I give Mary all my atoms she will plant them

in a garden where ripened women relinquish

their bones to make room for littler women.

It is dangerous to grow accustomed to a garden.

Just when the flowers soften you, they disappear.

Then you are a weepy fern among skyscrapers.

I don't want my soul exposed like that.

Neither can you make a garden stay. Don't even try.

Every plot becomes a dark city over time.

I have collected many dark ideas over time.

I have so many ideas they are a second coat.

PRISM DITCH

What I am saying is doomed:
men in tunnels running headfirst into trains
with grins on their faces.

Men lay out the wine and incense
for my memorial service.
I wanted there to be no wine
but I am dead.

I sleep on my hair like a wolf.
I knock against the shells
of cicada-men.

Have you ever crawled inside a shell?
It is the end of an image
you projected and adored.

The image was ripe
and full of protein
but people kept mouthing
the word *surrender*
which you must have heard
because you killed it.

I killed a pinkish man.
I popped the bubble of his head
with a safety pin.

This released a ticker
bleating *you you you you*
and all the ink
that poured from his mouth
I had written.

DAZE BONES

Notgod set me on fire and was like good luck

I think the shirt you wear is ultimate

When it turns red nothing can walk soft

Maybe birth me up on your fingers

You taste like not-sober alcoholics

Various breeds of errors and the way I feel you

No human power no human power

I cannot go there with you and I cried

The other life I was so nauseous

You didn't know I almost threw up

What if I threw up on your tongue?

When I put you in my mouth I got better

Forgive every body its mouth

I talk like I am sister heaven

I am really sister darkness

I am both at once and you are also

You didn't know you were an echo

In the dust I'll kill you up

I think you learn by unbeing

Like first you die and then go oh

SPIRIT FEAR

The room where I will die is everywhere
I am hiding from a signal on the road
Signal from the angels or signal from the mother
Signal from the dog who is a wolf who is me
Signal from myself that I gag not to hear
Signal from the Earth and under the Earth
And I hear the roar of the walls
I eat a young man in the room of my death
I make everyone into a lantern
I make pockets of darkness so the room looks like heaven
And I declare my love to the darkness
Its cocks and its holes like my cocks and my holes
Stick a rag in my mouth for my lover
Make the dead smell like the dead

FORGOTTEN NOTHING

Can you die with the Earth
yes I can die
green green grass make me make me

I am going to become something pure and true
I am built for becoming
though I was made came
I unknew my arrival because
I unknew the way

I say nobody knows the way besides the way
I say once was lost but now am lost

I say never asked to wake
please make the waking gentle
for this woke child with shut eyes

FROM

LAST
SEXT

I AM ABOUT TO BE HAPPY

Can you feel it?

You are art and you are not art

Yesterday I thought it was good to be dead

I babbled, a wildwoman boiling your pelt

I wore you as my t-shirt and mouth

I said it was good for you to be art

Save me from death, let me rise from the dead

Today I bury your body

LUNAR SHATTERS

I came into the world a young man

Then I broke me off

Still the sea and clouds are pegasus colors

My heart is pegasus colors but to get there I must go back

Back to the time before I was a woman

Before I broke me off to make a flattened lap

And placed therein a young man

Where I myself could have dangled

And how I begged him enter there

My broken young man parts

And how I let the mystery collapse

With rugged young man puncture

And how I begged him turn me pegasus colors

And please to put a sunset there

And gone forever was my feeling snake

And its place dark letters

And me the softest of all

And me so skinless I could no longer be naked

And me I had to debanshee

And me I dressed myself

I made a poison suit

I darned it out of myths

Some of the myths were beautiful

Some turned ugly in the making

The myth of the slender girl

The myth of the fat one

The myth of rescue

The myth of young men

The myth of the hair in their eyes

The myth of how beauty would save them

The myth of me and who I must become

The myth of what I am not

And the horses who are no myth

How they do not need to turn pegasus

They are winged in their unmyth

They holy up the ground

I must holy up the ground

I sanctify the ground and say fuck it

I say fuck it in a way that does not invite death

I say fuck it and fall down no new holes

And I ride an unwinged horse

And I unbecome myself

And I strip my poison suit

And wear my crown of fuck its

MY OWN NOTHING

I went under my skin

Which was my old skin

And under the skin of my soul

Which was an old soul

Though new to me

There was so much silence

I was surprised to like it

I saw that all my wounds were only dust

And when I turned to dust they would be vanished

And saw that I would have to be the mother

I have to be the tit and friend and child

And stroke my hairs and say peace

The hairs on my head and the hairs on my soul

They are bulbing in the rain

They look like crops and I am scared of them

Because one day they will be dust

And silence knows they will be dust

But what will become of silence

When everything else dusts

I have to know the silence will hold on to me

Know it not by head or by reflection

But touch it in the emptiness beneath my dust

Already returning me to light

COSMIC DITCH

I can't believe how much the darkness

Light is all the time but I see wrong

Will you be ok? asks the old god

You will be ok, says the new god

O I've been so darkness since the old god left

I've been purple incense

This is the shittiest part of the universe

Maybe it's the best

Tell me how to feel and I will feel it

Make me into a socket

I want to bleed electricity on the shadow of the world

I want to be zero

GLOWING LOSER

Neon coming from outside me cursed be

Light from the most high I want you

Ditches in my head I fall in every dawn

The bad soldiers in there want me corpsed

I am sorry soldiers

Get on your knees and become women

Become my women

Worship light and in doing so transform

Do not ask me how

Something has to do it for you

Something higher or other

An inner other

A sky in there

The good sky

Fall on your swords

Don't die

Become other

See you as the sky sees you

See me that way too

BONE ROOMS

Ladder to the genitals of god

You never go high enough

I guess the skull must have its purpose

Mine might even give me silence

Mostly I am full of names

Demetrius and Christopher and Daniel and John

Cemeteries built around those letters

I dig the dead boys up and try to dance

In my bedroom I am dancing with skeletons

A cotillion of cartilage and the meat of my life

I will let the meat rot for a pile of teeth

The world should forget me I am animating clavicles

Now I'm in the kitchen brining hip bones

There are femurs insulating all the walls

I am ribbing up the windows of the real

I am never getting over my mind

IN WANT OF RESCUE FROM THE REAL

My mindfriends went

They offed themselves

I made new mindfriends fast and wet

But they kept dying dry

Fantasies die so dry

Still I held on

Because the real is arctic

And I am without womb

And the char of inner Earth

Will ash my bones sometime

Then they all began to die

Before they even breathed

And I could see their corpses

Before I saw their eyes

And a thousand past-life deaths

Tore the mask off my mind

And I am scared of death

And I am scared of life

NECRO GLOW

Wreck my temporary wrists in the white of the sun

The sun says it is happiness but I get colder

And everything becomes a stairway to a hospital

And I from self to nature back to self

And dark is the dark of having to be a body

Daylife in the boneyard not my own

The cruel of the mind in the sack of the having to die

The sunlight laughing in my face because it knows

And everything goes tone-deaf when it is born

Deaf to the howls of the other side

Blind to the sane of the dead and dying

Sand on the mirror from my last life

Go there honey go under the ground

I who never wished to be free

I see freedom and I am mourning

The shadows of boys in the sun

They are forever and I am melting

Maybe I can be here just this once

Maybe I can eat the part that is dying

Maybe I'll shit out the minutes

I have been waiting to be split open

I wait for words from the other side

Wings should reveal themselves big and kind

Everyone is crying really hard

MAN'S SEARCH FOR MEANING

There is a lot of love and then there isn't

Then there is

I look to the shitdoors for love

Because they glitter

O the glittery shit

So much more magnetic than what

I have inside me

Inside me is more shit

But not glittery

Though below the shit is maybe a fucking temple

And when one shitdoor closes

You must build another shitdoor

From the dregs of reality and shitmind

O bless those dregs

With fantasy and therein

Lies your glitter

Yes, bless that glittery shitdoor

So much like the first door

But this door will be different really

Infinite shitdoors if you want them really

I want them

AMERICANS

Clocks are all that are coming to me

Better laugh back into childhood feeling

Before it is too gone

Yes I see a pink ocean overtake the clocks

Yes it is only a hallucination

And I don't know if the ocean has feelings for me

But the shadow of a boy keeps me safe

From me

Though the shadow

Is actually me

And when a warplane flies over the waves

I don't remember god

And when my childhood feeling surfaces

I kiss the shadow of my boyself

And eat sand

LIKE A REAL FLAME

I want the hole in my ear to be quiet

And inside the hole in my ear to be quiet

And I want it to tell me what to do

Or I will go to my lover's mouth

And say *oh my quiet*

I am coming

And tell the quiet how its kingdom should be made

Though the quiet has already eaten me

Because the quiet loves me

But does the lover love me

And why must the quiet be so quiet

And why can't the quiet have a cock

And where is its violet mouth

Its ten fingers with which to fix me

And where is its belly breathing

And O I want to be fixed

But I am already fixed

Why don't I feel it

BORING ANGEL

Now I know the trick is fantasy

I always knew it

But I didn't know the problem of bodies

Or I didn't know it entirely

How you must abandon the bones of the real

No angel wings projected on the ribcage

I had bloodstained sheets and I could not let go

I noosed myself on them in the woods

And hung there for eighteen days

Until I myself became an angel

Now I make love with no body

I do it with my halo chanting

Set me alive and fucking

A boy attached to no reality

He who needs no milk or punishing

He who will never abandon

How I love my celestial being

He who will never corpse

We are only air my seraphboy and me

Fucking with no eyes and flying

LIVING VOMIT

Sick people find each other and it is not a good thing

Sometimes it is a great thing

Every person is a sick person

Is that even true?

I lap your milk of illness up

It nurtures my dying

How bad am I doctor?

Very fatal, getting final

INNOCENT GROUND

Smeared in violent lipstick

A day with no boy in it

I don't touch reality

But I'm on the map of want

And here I am here I am

Jewbag plus some evil

And I dream you and I dream you

Eyefucks in the blanket

SKELETON GLITTER

The creepers are of the brain variety

The creepers are all me

Creep on me

Hello god

Why can't I be good

Shadow of the baby

Redemption of the soft friend

She said she would never

Leaving me

I walk through the wrong door

Pressed head and nothing is enough

I am looking for ways to get out

I am investigating

And I do remember the sky

I remember living up

If only I was blanked

The ground would give me a hug

Come in and wolf me

Enter the chambers and be them

Shipwreck and bathe in blank

We are talking serious baptism

And I know where not to go

And I know where not to go

And I run right to that place

And it's gleaming

INSTANT RAIN

Fall in all the wells at the same time

Yes I think I am having a human experience

I died in the mind

I died today

The blue sun in the blue sky like my face

My face could never hide anything

I went under my face and found curtains

I played a girl

LIQUID END

What you get is emptier

What you do is throw it all away

The lamb's blood on the door

Pestilence summer

Still your fingers smell of darkness

The darkness opens new holes

Let there be ditches

Let you die in ditches and never use again the body of
    another

The bruises you shall take with you and heal next life

Last life you were a locust

Last life you were a person

Ghosts of make-believe gods hanging around the television

No housecats

Jew of the salt and salty tastebuds

When your mother's hair falls out you will know

Roses weep for your future knowing

Find bones beneath the poolhouse of the world

The poolhouse indicates the pool is elsewhere

It is nearby but not on this planet

The bones are of god's dreampeople

The dreampeople are us

We are the ones who are supposed to be better

Something broke inside

Something was broken at conception

Now god fills with guilt

Now god cries for all of us

There is no punishment

Just the mother of suicide child

God wants to throw the stars back in the cauldron

Put down the receiver and start again

SALT

How can you go swimming in another human being?

I am swimming and asking for light

Once I paddled into dust and fucking

And the horsemen and ruin

And the poisonous hollows of a projected blue eye

And cracked my skull on all and caught more disease

In my already dreadmind and entered the medicines

Of no human power, the forests of disappearing moans

Which were rich in sap but lacked dissolve

Fertilized against my own swimming nature, Aleph

I am swimming for you now and I don't care

When you leave the forest you do not become the ocean

And I have become the desert trying to swim in the ocean

And knowing this, carrying the forest floor in a sweet
    wood coffin

And the blackbrush and rocks, the yucca and cacti of
    receded oceans

Which were never oceans at all or there would have

    been shells on the sand

They only looked like oceans in my thirst, I cut the old

    horizon

With a sword you have given and I gut the heavens

And bleed their light and swim in that

SENSATION OF IS

Horses in the night take me away from me and I am glad

In the morning my demon kingdom come again

Demon me demon head demon not enough and never

    enough

The trauma of this living is that it is real

Oh and then my casket lowers into the ground

And after that a navy sky and me alone in it

Me alone again with the stars

Me back to the blaze of ink the first one

Me just a tadpole and also made of everything

Like in the beginning and I remember all of it

The first forgetting how at birth they took me far from me

And how I was not glad to be taken

And I am told to stop thinking about dying

Ok fine then nothing

DUST MOAN

A love that should not exist on earth

I am in the wrong love or on the wrong planet

I am already heaven or maybe illusion

Can people tell how mirage I am?

How is love supposed to look and feel?

I half-ask god but am scared to hear

Hide the seams of prism children I am

So I do not have to kill them all

SPACE ORPHAN

When I get the shakes they spell M-O-T-H-E-R

I fill the world with blank vomit that I spew in blank

Sorry for the first tit in my mouth that didn't milk

Sorry I'm not yet the stars and in skin

A slum until the end I call it body

When ruin comes I'll hug me briefly

Then I'll dance around an astral fire in my skull

Then my bones will turn to silence I can't wait

ARE WE FEAR

The sky told me nothing about myself

The stars told me nothing about myself

Jupiter gave me zero

Except that I am dust

Which is a lot to go on

But not enough to stop the death

Where are we going to live?

I said to my unknown self

When one of us is dead

She did not say

But opened up a curtain

Where her silence lived

And I went behind the curtain

And laid my skeleton down

I lay in silence as she stroked my tired head

And then I heard a roaring crowd

And knew that I had been onstage

And knew that I was good

BIG TIDE

Nothing was made for me

I have to keep making it

Everything was made for me

The ocean, though I didn't know it till I murdered

What evil did I murder that I finally knew the ocean?

No evil no evil I simply saw the ocean

I saw the ocean for the first time

After having seen it for 2000 years

And when I finally saw the ocean

It murdered evil for me

You ask me to define evil

I don't know I can't

I can only say there are things that stand

In the way of other things

And the ocean murders all of them

BROKEN OCEAN

But then the water grows dark and recedes

I guess it is self-protection

To imagine the part where the water grows dark and recedes

As everything grows dark and recedes

I guess

I need a jumping-off point to this image

Love is the jumping-off point to this image

But love isn't even the water

Real love is the light

Don't you know that yet?

The water is something else

As anything that grows dark and recedes

Is something else not love

Fine then I don't want love

Fine then I don't want love

I want the water

CADAVER LAMB

When there is no one left

When it is just me and god

What do I say?

I say *help*

I say *freezing*

I say *I am wrong*

But god you never made me feel that way

Humans speak god

I am one of those humans

Many ugly things

Blood head skull hole

Milk mouth teeth rot

Sun hair dick suck

Mother water egg eye

Ugly and real

Ugly and real

I don't want to share

My life with anything real

God is real

I am trying to get better

What does that mean?

HE SHE

We were kissing in the pigs and fucking in the pigs

My god said it was not love

But my other god said it was

My god just wants me to be happy

And my other god wants me to be happy

And the women have not stopped crying

Throughout history

So I said kill me with your arrow cock

And I will cry too

Only later

LUNAR WIDOW

You will never be a centaur without me

But you will be a pilgrim

The stars don't give a shit

We should be under one piece of cloth

Maybe sleep on my hair across the continent

Watch me go up in the sky I do

Now I'm falling into the ocean

You gave me only drops of what I want

I wanted to haul

I wanted to harbor your wreck

Stop not blowing the conch

Be a childhood ok?

The heart so ready before it existed

My mouth on your silence

The dark of not getting what I want

The dark of getting it

Holes forever and ever

Shoes of the father so stepped on

The belly of our thing I don't know what it is

But I know something slit it

Call me a jellyfish

In the evening my body grows a penis

I want you in my odor

And I don't give a shit about the stars

I want your skin for a screen

I can project a cemetery

You can smoke all you want

Welcome to the coffin

MOON VIOLENCE

The peace I will not pray for

Silence I won't sit in

Zero surrender

The manbaby splayed for my affection

I say no

I ride an animal along the shore

Any animal

I have my knife and money

A throat

I am a woman and no woman at all

The honey drips I taste myself

I eat me in an arc on the water

Dig out my third eye

The hole I fill with sickness this time

Every time

This is what I do with love

LIQUID ARROWS

Let me give you the gift of dinner

The dinner is mine and it is not mine

It is our dinner and everybody's dinner

There are infinite dinners and there is only one dinner

I will give you the one

I ate at feasts with Bacchus

I ate wild boar and citrons

Brains in rose patina

Cherries, lambs, suckling pig, blood sausages and quinces

The water was cold and the wine seemed nice

Wine was going to be nice for a very long time

Then it would not be nice

I was nine, eleven, thirteen

My breasts came in and there were seven pubic hairs

    on my mound

Bacchus came and laced my cup with serum

A sleeping serum?

No a vomiting serum

In the field I felt that I would vomit

Bacchus sat me on his lap facing the sunset

My legs straddled his knee

The pressure of his knee and the pleasure of the coming
vomit

My seven pubic hairs

The hands of Bacchus clasped around my stomach

My stomach fat but Bacchus didn't care

So my stomach thin

Bacchus put his fingers down my throat to help the vomit
come

I burped and burped but nothing came

I burped like the ocean

I burped like quicksand

Bacchus gave me water to make the vomit come

When I vomited up the water he kept his hand in my mouth

The vomit went down his arm in a waterfall

The vomit bathed his body

I vomited down his arm all night

The vomit smelled like dead boar

It smelled like brains

It smelled like coins, gladiolus petals, mother's milk

    and cloudrealm

Bacchus said he wanted to hear my stomach scream

I screamed and screamed until I had no more screams

Then I began singing

This was joy

I RUN RIGHT THROUGH MYSELF AND DON'T CRACK

The ground under me is nothing

My tendons are nothing

The dick in my palace is nothing

My ancestors eaten by flames are nothing

The flames themselves are something

All my holes are something

Universe universe tell me my secret

The wind in your thoughts and the perfume in your heart

FORGOTTEN SOUND

I pretended the lust was voices

And I wrote down the voices

And sometimes the voices spoke as I had written them

To confirm what I already knew

Which is that I am a child and ready for petting

And sometimes the voices said nothing

To confirm what I already knew

Which is that I am filled with holes

And sometimes the voices said strange words

To confirm what I did not know

Which is that I am a ghost

And the men are real

And going on without me

INSIDE WORLD

Slices of paradise cut in because

Paradise demands our attention

My paradise is a coma I think

It hurts so much to keep walking

Sometimes comas brush against my feet

But I still love on Earth

And will maybe stay alive

Without everything I think I need

The angels are singing me to sleep

The dream of being alive gets born

I get scared and redream it

And everything I touch on Earth

Resembling angels

I try to eat

MAGIC ISN'T DEAD

All the seers predicted who I am

They said *she is a waiting room for bones*

Still I am after some non-predictable end

Where I go beyond skin and hair

I am a fuck demon in a fuck castle

Also electricity and no dust

And I am coming for you spirit

I am avenging everything

The gravestone they tried to make you in the rain

I will make the rain stop

Or I will make it rain animal bodies

And you will see your face in the lions

CHROME COUNTRY

And when you believe you are good

After you have felt wrong for a very long time

The angels come find you and blow in your eyes

And you become a glowing fish

And all of your tears turn to ocean

And the iron world rolls backward

And there in space you are saved

From yourself and also the future

And a quiet voice is all that there is

There in space and floating above it

There in your gills and also your lungs

A quiet voice is all that there is

LAST SEXT

Am I crying on coal mountain

The sky is a funnel I want it

I want to be sucked by the moon

Or needled into the night

Or into the eye of a cock

Of a boy with a mouth like mine

And together we enter a door in the sky

Which is one door

But all doors

And the breath there is his but mine

And the truth in the door is many

As the truth on coal mountain is many

But also one truth alone

A truth I have felt since always

Before the time of the cock

Do I point to it from my sickbowl

Perched high atop coal mountain

And I can never say its name

As I gape into the dark

And see the jaw of a boy

Reflected in my sickbowl

My bowl of gristle and blood

My thoughts of bellies and scythes

And how to cut me out of me

The vine of the mind and the heart and its sword

And the smoke of the coals in the dark

And his hands on my dress and his mouth on my death

And the bites of want in the dawn

When the boy disappears with the sun

How his body becomes a soot

And his semen dissolves in the wind

But his shadow remains on coal mountain

Am I mine

LONG TOMB

My pussy tastes like rain to you

I will not make this a romantic poem

Poems are made of mistakes

Poems about poetry are mistakes

I look to mistakes and say *am I ok?*

I look to mistakes and say *make me ok*

My pussy tastes like pussy

And I have been scared since the day I was born

HOW I GET OVER MY LIFE

I turn my mind to bread and feed it to dogs

The dogs are good of stars and never devils

They eat me into something better maybe a door

They eat me to a sky until I'm gone from me

They swallow all my voices cold and drill

They hollow me out for all the good secrets

The secrets give me third eye until sunrise

I shut my mouth the whole time

I'M COMING

The people talked to me of god

Then god talked to me of god

God said *do not move*

I said *I know*

And then got very still and knew that I was not

And saw our shadows in the room

Two wild and kindly dogs

Leaking light from out their wet jaws

The good of breath from where we all began

Though our minds try to tell a different story

A tale of man and his machete

Murder of our dogs when we fake being men

Or live a lifetime in the human codes

Fierce we cut the shadows with our seeing-eye bones

Gently then we dress the wounds

In nothing

That will lead us back to Earth

ACKNOWLEDGMENTS

Much love and gratitude to Meredith Kaffel Simonoff, Tony Perez, Jakob Vala, Elizabeth DeMeo, Becky Kraemer, Nanci McCloskey, Yashwina Canter, Alyssa Ogi, Craig Popelars, Matthew Dickman, and everyone else behind the scenes at Tin House, Adam Robinson, Jason Cook, Ruth Curry, Emily Gould, Laia Garcia-Furtado, Daniel Lopatin, Dorothea Lasky, Patricia Lockwood, Elaine Equi, David Groff, Leigh Hovey, my parents Robert and Linda Broder, my sister Hayley Broder, and always, Nicholas.

*

Grateful acknowledgment is made to the editors of the following publications, where some of these poems first appeared:

Action Yes; Adult; *The Atlas Review*; The Awl; *Bluestem*; *BOMB*; *Books & Culture*; *Coconut*; The Collagist; *Columbia Journal*; Court Green; *DEATH HUMS*; *Denver Quarterly*; *FENCE*; Flavorwire; Ghost Proposal; *Gigantic*; *glitterMOB*; Guernica; HTMLGIANT; *Illuminati Girl Gang*; *The Iowa Review*; Lamination Colony; Loaded Bicycle; *Lo-Ball*; *LUNGFULL!*; The Morning News; NewHive; *NOÖ Journal*; On Earth As It Is; *PANK*; Paperbag; PEN; *Ping-Pong Free Press*; POETRY; Poets.org; Powder Keg; Rhizome; Sixth Finch; *The Third Rail Quarterly*; *Tin House*; Typo; The Volta; *Washington Square Review*; *Women's Studies Quarterly*; *Yalobusha Review*